What Is My Fault?

A Pastoral Reflection on Innocent Suffering and the Voice of Job

Rev. Joe Varghese

February 2026

ISBN 978-1-7644924-0-9

Published by:

Joe Varghese

Printed and distributed by IngramSpark

Printed in Australia

To my mother,

whose strength and faith guided me every step of
the way.

Table of Contents

Foreword

One of the most persistent and heartfelt questions I have encountered during my 33 years of full-time ministry is this: Why does God allow pain and suffering? It is a question that has echoed through hospital rooms, counselling sessions, and quiet conversations with those searching for meaning in the midst of hardship. This book addresses this very issue with clarity, compassion, and deep theological insight.

Pain and suffering are universal experiences. No one escapes them, and yet the purpose behind them remains one of life's greatest mysteries. Father Joe recognises this struggle and approaches it head-on, offering readers a clear understanding of a topic that has confounded many for centuries. His writing is both accessible and profound, making complex theological truths understandable without sacrificing depth.

What sets this book apart is its unwavering focus on the hope found in the Christian faith. Father Joe demonstrates how, even in the darkest valleys, the promises of God bring peace and assurance. He reminds us that suffering is not meaningless; rather, it can be a pathway to growth, compassion, and deeper trust in God's goodness. This perspective is not theoretical—it is deeply practical, offering comfort to those who are hurting and guidance to those who minister to them.

Father Joe does not shy away from comparing the Christian understanding of suffering with other worldviews. He clearly shows how alternative philosophies often fall short, either denying the reality of pain or failing to provide any ultimate purpose for it. In contrast, the Christian narrative offers a framework that acknowledges suffering while pointing to redemption and hope beyond this life.

For pastors, counsellors, and anyone walking alongside those in pain, this book is an invaluable resource. It equips readers with answers that are both intellectually satisfying and spiritually comforting. For those personally wrestling with suffering, it offers a lifeline—a reminder that pain does not have the final word.

Father Joe's book is a pastoral guide for a hurting world. It speaks to the heart as much as to the mind, reaffirming that in Christ, even suffering can be redeemed. If you have ever asked, 'Why pain?' or walked with someone who has, this book is a must-read.

Rev. Andrew Tokin
Church of Christ

Acknowledgement

This book is my first offering, and I begin with gratitude to Almighty God. It is by His grace alone that this work has come to completion. In seasons of study, reflection, doubt, and perseverance, He has been faithful. Whatever is true, helpful, and edifying in these pages is a testimony to His sustaining presence and enabling strength.

I am sincerely thankful to Angela Hung for her prayers, encouragement, and steady support. Her perceptive inputs and readiness to engage with this work have been a quiet encouragement throughout its development.

I am deeply thankful to Rev. Andrew Tokin for graciously writing the foreword and for his generous encouragement throughout this journey. His steady support and confidence in this work have been a gift.

My sincere appreciation goes to Rev. Phillip Zamagias and his dear wife, Leeanne. Their careful reading, thoughtful corrections, and valuable insights have strengthened this work in significant ways. I am grateful for their time, clarity, and kindness.

I am also especially thankful to Rev. Simon Robinson for his generous support, time, and constructive feedback. His thoughtful engagement with my ideas, pastoral wisdom, and willingness to challenge and refine my arguments have enriched this work considerably.

As this book grew out of my pre-doctoral paper, I owe a special debt of gratitude to Rev. Dr. Thomas Kattathra, S.J., for his scholarly guidance and steady mentorship. His intellectual rigour and patient direction challenged me to think more deeply, write more clearly, and pursue theological reflection with integrity.

Finally, I wish to thank my wife for her support during my studies. Her prayers and sacrifices sustained me through long hours of reading and writing.

To all who have walked with me in this season, I offer my heartfelt thanks.

Preface

What This Book Is and Is Not

This book is not a commentary on the Book of Job. It is also not an attempt to solve the problem of suffering. Many theologians have already done that work, and their insights are valuable. What follows is something simpler and more personal.

This book grew out of pastoral encounters. I have sat with people whose suffering could not be explained. Their pain could not be turned into meaning. It could not be redeemed with answers. In those moments, I learned that what was needed was not explanation, but presence. Not resolution, but honesty before God.

Job appears throughout these pages, not as a text to be fully unpacked, but as a companion in faith. His story shows us that Scripture does not rush to defend God. It does not protect us from the shock of unanswered suffering. Even when God speaks, He does not give Job a clear explanation for his pain. Instead, He calls Job to humility and trust in the midst of mystery.

This book refuses the temptation to tidy suffering into doctrine. It names a hard truth: life is difficult, suffering is real, and faith does not exempt us from pain.

If you are looking for answers, this book may disappoint.

If you are looking for permission to be faithful without clarity, honest without certainty, and reverent without resolution, then I hope these reflections will serve you well.

Author's Note

The reason for writing this book is not only academic but deeply personal. During my Bachelor of Theology studies, I was given an opportunity to travel to Mumbai. One of my batchmates was working with Bombay Teen Challenge, an organisation with a strong presence in red-light areas. Their ministry focused on women involved in commercial sex work and on caring for their children. During my visit, I was taken into one of these areas and introduced to the work being done there.

On one occasion, I was brought into a brothel to meet the owners. While we were speaking, a young woman came and sat nearby. The owners mentioned that she was from my hometown. I was given some time to speak with her privately. We spoke for a while, and she asked me why I was involved in ministry. I shared my faith with her, and she listened carefully. Then I asked her, "Why are you here? What is your story?"

She explained that she had been living with her family and had fallen in love with a man whom her family did not approve of. He persuaded her to leave home with the promise of marriage. After travelling to Mumbai and staying briefly with acquaintances, she awoke one morning to find herself in a brothel. She was informed that she had been sold and would not be free until a debt was repaid. She spoke of ongoing abuse and exploitation, and of a body and spirit worn down by suffering.

This was my first time inside a brothel, my first conversation with a woman involved in sex work, and my first time hearing such a painful and unbearable story. Before we parted, she asked me a question that I was not prepared for. She said, "If your God is loving, caring, and powerful, why has this happened to me? What did I do wrong? Why am I being punished, and not the man who sold me?"

For the first time, I had no answer. I simply remained silent and listened. From that moment on, the question of innocent suffering began to burn deeply within me.

Over time, I visited hospitals and met people who were dying. I met husbands who had lost their wives, wives who had lost their husbands, children who had lost their parents, and parents who had lost their children. Again and again, the same question returned: why do innocent people suffer?

After my graduation, I returned to Mumbai to serve God in ministry. During this time, I learned that the woman I had spoken with in the brothel had died. Her death marked a turning point in my life. From that point onward, my ministry took a new direction. I became involved in social justice work, particularly in efforts to rescue minors and adults forced into prostitution, to support families trapped in bonded labour, and to protect children exploited through child labour.

This book is a reflection shaped by my life and ministry, lived in the presence of suffering. It does not offer easy answers. Instead, it seeks to listen carefully to Scripture, to human experience, and to the mystery of God's presence in pain. The question of suffering remains complex, but through these encounters, I have come to believe that faith is not about explaining suffering away, but about standing with those who suffer and trusting God even when answers are not clear.

General Introduction

Suffering is something none of us can completely escape. It reaches into the body, the mind, and the spirit, often all at once. Sometimes it hits like a storm, sudden and overwhelming. At other times, it lingers in the background, a dull ache that colours daily life. It is not only individuals who suffer, but whole families, communities, and even entire nations can be marked by it. There are many reasons why people suffer. It can be the result of cruelty or injustice. Sometimes we bring it upon ourselves through choices we regret. And then, there are those moments that are the hardest to understand, when suffering falls on people who did nothing to deserve it. Suffering is not always easy to put into words. Some people cry out. Others fall silent. Pain can speak through a trembling voice or the absence of speech. It shows up in the body, in tears, and in sleepless nights.

Every major religion wrestles with the question of suffering, offering different frameworks through which to understand it. In Hinduism, suffering is often linked to *karma*, the consequences of actions, whether in this life or a previous one. It is seen not simply as punishment, but as part of a moral and cosmic order that shapes the soul's journey.

In Buddhism, suffering, or *dukkha*, is viewed as an inherent part of life, arising from desire, attachment, and ignorance. The path to liberation lies in understanding and transcending these root causes. In Islamic theology, suffering is interpreted through the lens of divine will. Everything that happens is under the sovereign decree of *Allah*, and even hardship can be a test, a purification, or a means of drawing closer to God.

Christianity, too, has its distinctive voice in this conversation. It proclaims that God is omniscient, omnipotent, omnipresent, and most of all, loving. However, this affirmation leads to an unavoidable and haunting question: If God truly sees all, knows all, holds all power, and loves without limit, why does suffering persist? Why do innocent people bear burdens they never chose? Why are children afflicted with pain they cannot understand? Why is evil allowed to flourish at all? These are not merely intellectual puzzles for theologians. They are the aching, personal cries of countless human beings. The question is not abstract. It is urgent. It comes from hospital beds and funeral homes, from war zones and quiet, lonely bedrooms. It comes from parents who have buried children, from survivors of abuse, from people who have prayed for healing and watched it not come.

The focus of this book takes its foundation from the Book of Job. Job is portrayed as an innocent man, righteous, blameless, and God-fearing, yet he is subjected to unimaginable suffering. Of all the books in Scripture, Job is the one most closely associated with the question of innocent suffering. Alongside the Book of Lamentations and the Passion narratives in the Gospels, Job stands as one of the most intense and probing reflections on the human experience of pain.

While Lamentations speaks of national grief, it speaks of Israel's suffering in the aftermath of Jerusalem's destruction. In comparison, Job brings the question down to the level of the individual. His story is personal. It unfolds through a series of dialogues that give voice to both theological reasoning and raw, emotional protest. Job becomes a symbol, not of punishment, but of mystery. He speaks for those who suffer without knowing why.

The Book of Job is widely believed to be one of the oldest books in the Bible. It carries within it echoes of Ancient Near Eastern thought, especially around suffering and divine justice. The worldview of that time was shaped heavily by what scholars call retribution theology. Retribution theology is a belief that the righteous are rewarded and the wicked are punished. Job's story unsettles that framework. It does not fit. Here is a man declared righteous by God Himself, yet stripped of everything: his family, his wealth, his health, without cause.

Throughout the book, Job's companions, Eliphaz, Bildad, Zophar, and later Elihu, offer explanations rooted in traditional wisdom. They insist that Job must have sinned. That suffering always has a moral cause. That God would not allow the innocent to suffer without reason. However, Job resists this. He does not claim to be perfect, but he refuses to accept the idea that his suffering is deserved. His cries are not only emotional but also theological.

He demands to understand. He speaks directly to God, challenging, pleading, grieving. Moreover, though God eventually responds, it is not with the answers Job expected.

Instead, God offers a deeper vision of divine wisdom, one that transcends human logic and control.

Over the centuries, many have tried to explain Job's suffering. Several interpretive models have emerged: the retribution theory, which the book critiques; the wager theory, where Satan challenges God's trust in Job's integrity; the idea that suffering serves as a means of purification or correction; and the view that Job's suffering ultimately serves a higher divine purpose to reveal the glory of God. Each of these perspectives captures something of the mystery, but none of them explains everything. Perhaps Job's story is not about solving the problem of suffering, but about teaching us how to walk through it with honesty, with courage, and with faith.

If suffering is inevitable, does the Bible offer a response that speaks to more than just the intellect? This is not a question raised only in academic debate. It is the question of the sick, the grieving, the abandoned. It is the question that rises when prayers seem unanswered and when even faith feels quiet. The biblical response to suffering is not a quick solution. It is not always a reason why. What it offers is something more lasting. It offers a God who listens, a God who speaks, and a God who stays.

The focus of this book is on those who endure suffering despite their innocence. Often, this pain comes from family, friends, or loved ones, making it deeply personal and challenging. Christianity is not a bed of roses, and being a believer does not exempt anyone from trials or hardship. Even faithful Christians can face undeserved suffering. Therefore, this book is for all who are suffering, exposed to harsh and inhumane conditions, often characterised by physical abuse, psychological trauma, and social marginalisation.

This pattern of exploitation is not random but is ingrained within larger systems of inequality and power imbalance. Women, children, and those from economically or socially marginalised communities are disproportionately affected. In many instances, victims are denied access to justice, deprived of legal identity, and stripped of the basic human dignity that affirms their status as persons created in the image of God.

Biblical theology speaks meaningfully to the reality of such suffering. The Scriptures consistently affirm that God is neither indifferent to human pain nor silent in the face of injustice. The Book of Job offers a complementary and complex theological reflection on suffering, especially the suffering of the innocent. His story challenges the dominant assumption within ancient wisdom literature that suffering is always the consequence of sin or wrongdoing.

The purpose of this work is to explore the underlying reasons for Job's suffering as presented in the biblical text and to analyse Job's response to that suffering. This book approaches Job thematically and pastorally rather than as a verse-by-verse exegetical commentary, focusing on reading Job in a way that speaks to the lived experience of suffering rather than settling every academic debate.

Through careful exegesis, the study will consider the theological, ethical, and existential dimensions of suffering as reflected in Job's experience, and how these insights might inform pastoral care, advocacy, and theological reflection in contemporary contexts.

The methodology is primarily theological and pastoral, using selected passages of Job to explore key themes and concepts, with attention to the original Hebrew where necessary. It is written for a general reader and aims to remain faithful to the text while maintaining readability.

This book is divided into three chapters. The first chapter offers a broad overview of the concept of suffering from both secular and ancient Hebrew perspectives. It begins by examining the understanding of suffering in the broader context of the Ancient Near East, considering cultural, religious, and social factors that shaped early views on human affliction. The chapter then narrows its focus to the pre-exilic period of Israel's history, highlighting how suffering was interpreted during this formative time. Finally, it explores the Deuteronomistic history, analysing the theological framework that links suffering with covenantal faithfulness and divine retribution. Through this multi-layered approach, the chapter seeks to provide a foundation for understanding the evolution of suffering in the Old Testament.

The second chapter centres specifically on the Book of Job and the nature of Job's suffering. It aims to explore the complex reasons behind Job's affliction as presented in the text, addressing the tension between innocence and suffering that Job's story embodies. This chapter critically engages with various scholarly interpretations and theological perspectives on Job's suffering, including traditional views such as retributive justice, as well as more contemporary readings that challenge conventional assumptions. Furthermore, the chapter offers a theological reflection on how Job's experience informs a Christian response to suffering today. It considers pastoral implications and how Job's story can provide both solace and challenge to those who endure unjust suffering in contemporary contexts.

Chapter Three reflects on how Christians respond to suffering, especially when it comes without explanation or fault. Using the story of Job as its guide, the chapter listens carefully to common Christian beliefs that try to make sense of pain, while recognising how easily these explanations can wound those who are already hurting. Rather than offering neat answers, the chapter invites readers to see suffering as a place where faith is tested not only by endurance, but also by honesty, trust, and hope. By bringing Job into conversation with the New Testament, it offers a response to suffering that neither denies pain nor glorifies it, but points to a God who remains present, faithful, and compassionate in the midst of human brokenness.

The scope of this book is centred on developing a pastoral response and practical application for addressing and understanding the experiences of innocent sufferers. This work seeks to offer theological insights and pastoral strategies that can support, empower, and advocate for individuals subjected to these forms of injustice, to foster healing, restoration, and justice.

Suffering is a complex and multifaceted topic that encompasses a wide range of perspectives and disciplines. This book does not attempt to provide an exhaustive or comprehensive outlook of suffering in its entirety. The research is limited to an examination of the Book of Job as a primary biblical text addressing the experience of suffering.

All citations in this work follow the Turabian style for footnotes and bibliography. Biblical quotations are taken from the New King James Version, unless otherwise noted.

With this broad understanding of suffering, the book now turns to the Old Testament, where ancient perspectives on affliction, justice, and divine providence take shape, leading to the profound and challenging story of Job.

Chapter One: Approaches to Understanding Suffering

It is theologically significant that the Bible does not shy away from the reality of human suffering but instead places it at the very centre of the biblical narrative. From the cries of lament in the Psalms to the misery of the prophets, from the suffering of Job to the afflictions of Christ and the early church, Scripture bears honest and sacred witness to the full range of human pain. In doing so, it affirms that suffering is not an anomaly in the life of faith, but a condition deeply connected to the fallen state of humanity and to the crying out of creation under the weight of sin.

Throughout Scripture, we see that suffering is not simply a personal or isolated experience. It is a universal human reality that touches every dimension of life: body, mind, heart, and soul. The effects of suffering extend beyond the individual, disrupting families, communities, and societies. On the other hand, suffering confronts us with theological questions that reach into the very nature of God's justice, providence, and presence. The biblical witness does not offer easy answers or philosophical abstractions. Suffering in Scripture is not merely a problem to be solved, but a place of encounter.

The reality of suffering is not unique to any one tradition but is addressed across the spectrum of world religions. Each offers its own framework for interpreting the origin, meaning, and purpose of suffering. In Hinduism, which embraces a polytheistic worldview, suffering is often linked to the concept of *karma*, the belief that one's present pain is the consequence of actions committed in a previous life. This cyclical understanding connects suffering to moral cause and effect across lifetimes. Buddhism, while non-theistic in its nature, teaches that suffering arises from desire, attachment, and ignorance. Therefore, the path to liberation lies in the discontinuation of these cravings through practices that lead to enlightenment.

In Islam, suffering is understood within the sovereign will of *Allah*. *Allah* permits suffering or hardship, and Muslims are encouraged to submit to God's decree with patience and trust. Questioning divine intent is generally discouraged, as submission to *Allah's* will is a fundamental expression of faith. Suffering, then, is a test, a means of spiritual purification, or a reminder of human dependence on the Creator.

In Christianity, while also affirming the sovereignty of God, it offers a distinct perspective on suffering that has sparked deep theological inquiry. Central to the Christian worldview is the belief that God is omniscient (all-knowing), omnipotent (all-powerful), omnipresent (all-present), and omnibenevolent (all-loving/good). This very understanding invites one of the most challenging questions in Christian theology: If God is all-powerful and all-loving, why does evil continue to exist? Why do both the righteous and the unrighteous suffer? Why does a good and sovereign God allow pain, injustice, and tragedy to continue?

Unlike many religious systems that view suffering as either fated, karmic, or purely internal, the Christian Scriptures root the origin of suffering in the misuse of human freedom. According to the biblical narrative, God blessed humanity with the freedom to choose, and through the fall, sin entered the world, distorting creation and introducing suffering and death. Christianity does not end the conversation there. Rather than merely diagnosing the problem, it presents a God who enters into human suffering through the incarnation of Jesus Christ. God does not remain distant from pain but bears it, redeems it, and promises a future in which all suffering will be wiped away. Thus, for Christians, the question of suffering is not just a philosophical dilemma but a deeply theological and pastoral concern.

To deepen our understanding of suffering, it is helpful to consider various categories that reflect its diverse causes and expressions. One form is self-imposed suffering. This type of suffering arises from an individual's own choices, whether intentional or accidental. This kind of suffering may stem from moral failure, unwise decisions, or continual patterns of behaviour that lead to personal harm. Though often preventable, this suffering still holds spiritual significance, as Scripture frequently points to God's redemptive work even in the consequences of human error.

A second category is innocent suffering, which refers to the pain endured by individuals through no fault of their own. This suffering can result from the cruelty or injustice of others, or from natural disasters, diseases, and circumstances beyond human control. Theologically, this type of suffering raises profound questions about divine justice and providence. The Bible does not ignore these questions, but instead confronts them openly.

The third type is vicarious suffering, a deeply theological concept found throughout Scripture. This form of suffering occurs when one chooses to suffer on behalf of another, voluntarily bearing pain or burden for the sake of someone else's good. In all forms, suffering calls us into a deeper awareness of human frailty, divine mercy, and the hope of redemption.

Even though suffering cannot be universally defined, it is expressed in ways that others can recognise, both verbally and nonverbally. The expression of suffering is basically subjective, as only the person experiencing it can truly describe its nature. This experience is not limited to physical or emotional pain alone but encompasses the entire being, influencing a person's thoughts, emotions, body, and overall sense of self.[1]

R. S. Wallace describes suffering as an "intrusion," a foreign element that entered the created order only after the fall of

---

[1] Cf. Dimitrios G. Oreopoulos, "Is There Meaning In Suffering?," in *Humane Medicine*, vol. 5, no. 2 (2005): 1.

humanity. This understanding is firmly rooted in Genesis 1:31, where Scripture declares, "God saw everything that He had made, and indeed, it was very good," a statement that affirms the perfection and harmony of the original creation, untouched by pain or death. Suffering, therefore, is not fundamental to creation itself, but is a tragic distortion, the result of sin breaking the relationship between God, humanity, and the world. It is experienced in a multitude of forms: conflict, injustice, disease, exploitation, alienation, and death.[2]

A proper understanding of suffering begins with discerning its root cause. Without grasping why suffering exists, any attempt to interpret its meaning or respond to it remains incomplete. Thus, to comprehend the nature of suffering, one must first confront the reality of the fall and the fractured state of a world that no longer reflects its original goodness.

---

[2] Cf. R. S. Wallace, "Suffering," in *New Bible Dictionary*, 3rd ed., eds. D. R. W. Wood and I. Howard Marshall (Leicester, England: InterVarsity Press, 1996), 1136.

1.1   Cause of Suffering: A Secular Perspective

From a secular standpoint, suffering is not typically viewed through the lens of sin or moral failure, as it often is within religious traditions. Instead, it is commonly understood as a natural or circumstantial phenomenon. It arises from human error, carelessness, environmental factors, social injustice, or simply the unpredictable and uncontrollable forces of nature. In this view, suffering does not necessarily carry spiritual meaning or moral consequence; rather, it is seen as an inevitable aspect of the human condition in a complex, at times indifferent universe.

Building on this outlook, Ulrich Diehl offers a framework for classifying suffering based on its external conditions, examining how individuals experience pain and hardship in response to factors beyond their internal moral or spiritual life, such as accidents, disasters, illness, or societal structures that perpetuate harm. The classification of suffering according to Diehl is as follows:

> People may suffer from a variety of circumstances, such as (a) harmful natural conditions (earthquakes, volcanic eruptions and bush fires, hurricanes, tornados and other extreme weather conditions), (b) harmful ecological conditions (radioactive or

chemical contamination of the atmosphere and landscape in a certain geographic region including people, animals and plants, food and water, or biological contamination with viruses or bacteria causing epidemics), (c) harmful political conditions (dictatorship or anarchy, war or terrorist attacks, bad government, the absence of a modern constitution and a legal state which guarantees basic human rights, law and order), (d) harmful economic conditions (lack of economic growth, unemployment and inflation, the untamed globalisation of the market, evasive international companies, lack of social and economic responsibility within management, the weakening of the political power of national governments), (e) harmful social conditions (inability to satisfy basic human needs, such as hunger and thirst, hygiene, shelter and clothing, security from aggression and crime), (f) harmful emotional conditions (inability to satisfy one's emotional needs for company, belonging and acceptance, the need for decent work, perspectives for one's future and self-respect through the freedom of self-determination), (g) harmful cognitive and spiritual conditions (inability to understand the natural and social world we live in, the inability to understand the *conditio humana,* i.e. the special position of human beings within the world equipped with the abilities for the acquisition of language and thought, of communication and community, of labor and cooperation, of love and self-transcendence through labor, art, science and religion), and (h) inability to experience and grasp some meaning of life.[3]

According to this school of thought, evil and suffering arise mainly when people fail to care for one another. When concern and empathy are absent, the dignity of the other person is overlooked, and harmful actions become easier to justify. The belief that "the end justifies the means" reflects this moral failure, as it allows people to excuse suffering in pursuit of personal gain or perceived greater goals. From a theological and pastoral perspective, such thinking reflects a broken understanding of love and responsibility, where self-interest replaces compassion and leads to further harm within the human community.

Secularists reject the belief in a deity who governs the universe and punishes humanity. They also do not accept the idea that suffering is a form of punishment or a test, as many religions teach. Within Humanism, the concept of "original sin," a Christian doctrine, is dismissed as unjust and cruel since it holds people accountable for the sins of their ancestors. The secularists' perspective does not claim that all

---

[3] Ulrich Diehl, "Human Suffering as a Challenge for the Meaning of Life," *An International Journal in Philosophy, Religion, Politics, and the Arts* 4, no. 2 (Fall 2009): 37.

humans are naturally sinful or flawed. However, it acknowledges that human beings can be aggressive and self-centred, making evil and suffering unavoidable realities.

Since suffering is unavoidable, the focus is to learn how to adapt to suffering rather than expecting it to be eliminated. The idea of God is mainly rejected because such a deity is seen as incapable of preventing evil and suffering from existing in the world.

Epicurus, an ancient Greek philosopher, taught that the highest good in life is the pursuit of happiness, which he understood primarily as the absence of pain and mental disturbance: a state he called *ataraxia* (tranquillity or peace of mind). Epicurus famously posed a challenge to the concept of God's nature by asking: If God is willing to prevent evil but lacks the power, then He is not omnipotent; if He has the power but is unwilling, then He is malevolent; if He is both willing and able, then why does evil exist; and if He is neither willing nor able, then why call Him God?[4]

---

[4] *The Ante-Nicene Fathers: Fathers of the Third and Fourth Century*, eds. Alexander Roberts, James Donaldson, and Arthur Cleveland Coxe, vol. 7 (New York: Cosimo, Inc., 2007), 271.

This line of reasoning exposes the tension between the reality of suffering and the traditional attributes ascribed to God. From this perspective, the apparent absence of divine intervention in suffering calls for a practical response rooted not in divine providence but in human responsibility. Without reliance on God, the approach to suffering emphasises its reduction and prevention through the pursuit of happiness, considered the highest good. Thus, ethical living and human well-being become central to facing pain and hardship in a world where divine justice is questioned.

In a worldview that excludes the presence and sovereignty of God, the challenge of suffering is approached through human effort and practical means. Without appeal to divine intervention or providence, the focus turns to easing pain and minimising hardship by fostering conditions that lead to human well-being and happiness. Happiness, understood here as the highest attainable good, becomes the guiding principle for addressing suffering. This approach emphasises the responsibility of humanity to create environments where joy, peace, and flourishing can flourish despite the presence of suffering. Although this human-centred response offers valuable strategies for coping, it also raises profound questions about the ultimate source of hope, meaning, and justice in the face of pain. It invites reflection on whether the pursuit of happiness alone can fully satisfy the deepest longings of the human soul or if there is a transcendent dimension to suffering and redemption that lies beyond mere mitigation.[5]

From a health point of view, suffering often shows through health-related challenges, influenced by a complex interplay of both external and internal factors. As H. Robert Silverstein notes, diseases cannot be solely attributed to stress, as many serious health conditions have clear and identifiable causes. Conditions such as hypertension, diabetes, elevated cholesterol, gallstones, and cancers affecting organs like the colon, prostate, and breast arise from a variety of direct influences. These include environmental factors like pollution in the air we breathe and water we consume, changes and contaminants in our food, sedentary lifestyles

---

[5] Cf. "Evil and Suffering," *Humanism for Schools*, accessed May 22, 2018, http://www.humanismforschools.org.uk/pdfs/evil%20and%20suff ering.pdf.

marked by insufficient physical activity, and sometimes unrealistic or harmful expectations placed upon the body.[6]

Even with significant progress in medical science, humans remain vulnerable to illnesses, whether they are contagious or not. Being vulnerable reminds us how fragile we truly are. No matter how healthy someone appears, they can still face unexpected health challenges. This fact reveals a core aspect of the human experience and encourages us to be humble and recognise our need for support. It also helps us accept our physical limits while inspiring a hopeful perspective that goes beyond the body, especially during uncertain times.[7]

From a health perspective, acknowledging the complexity of factors contributing to illness rightly reminds us of human vulnerability and limitation. Even in this context, the secular view may fall short in addressing the psychological and spiritual suffering that accompanies physical illness. The awareness of mortality and fragility often leads to existential questions that science alone cannot resolve.

---

[6] Cf. H. Robert Silverstein, "How Virtually All Diseases Occur," *The Preventive Medicine Center*, accessed May 22, 2018, http://www.thepmc.org/2010/04/how-virtually-all-diseases-occur/

[7] Cf. H. Wheeler Robinson, *Suffering Human and Divine* (New York: The Macmillan Company, 1939), 6.

1.2   Cause of Suffering: A Hebrew Perspective

From the Hebrew worldview, God, as the Creator, did not design the world to be a place of pain and sorrow. On the contrary, creation was originally brought into being in a state of perfect harmony and flourishing, as clearly portrayed in the opening chapters of Genesis. This world, in its initial form, reflected the goodness and intentional order of God's creative will. This harmony has been derailed and is now deeply missed, a condition that calls for careful examination.

To understand why suffering entered a world that was once flawless, one must engage with the Hebraic interpretation of human disobedience, relational disconnection, and the consequences of moral freedom. This perspective reveals that suffering is not a random or inevitable part of existence but the result of a profound breach in the divine-human relationship, which distorts the original peace and balance intended by God.

1.2.1 Ancient Near East Perspective

Within the Judaic tradition, suffering is commonly understood as the result of breaking the Law of God, whether by an individual or a community. This perspective is deeply rooted in the broader worldview of the Ancient Near East, which shaped early Jewish thought. A clear example of this is found in John 9:2, where the disciples ask Jesus, "Rabbi, who sinned, this man or his parents, that he was born blind?" This question reflects a longstanding belief in the early Judaic mindset that suffering could precede a person's birth and might be linked to sins committed by previous generations. In this view, suffering is not simply a personal misfortune but is often understood as a consequence inherited from the actions of the first human ancestors, passed down through generations.[8]

The concept of suffering being closely connected to the sins of the first human parents appears repeatedly throughout the Hebrew scriptures, as well as in the New Testament and intertestamental writings. This understanding, often referred to as retribution theology, views suffering as a direct and purposeful response from God to the moral failings of an

---

[8] The notion of innocent suffering due to ancestral sin is found in Ex 20:5-7; Deut 5:9-10 and Num 14:18. These cursed-based-spell-sin of parents is also carried through child birth, as psalmist said, "The wicked are estranged from the womb; They go astray as soon as they are born, speaking lies" (Ps 58:3).which is seen in Gen 25:22, "But the children struggled together within her." Cf. Grant Osborne and Philip W. Comfort, *Cornerstone Biblical Commentary*, vol. 13 (Illinois: Tyndale House Publishers, 2007), 142.

individual, a community, or even an entire nation. In this framework, suffering is not random but serves as a form of divine justice, revealing the intimate relationship between human actions and their consequences under God's sovereign rule.[9]

According to the worldview of the Ancient Near East, as noted by Greg W. Parsons, wisdom is grounded in the belief that there is a deep and inherent unity between all aspects of the cosmos. This worldview affirms that the natural world and the moral or social order are not separate realms but are closely connected. What occurs in nature is seen to reflect, or even influence, what unfolds in human society and ethical behaviour. This perspective is clearly echoed in the speech of Bildad in the Book of Job, who appeals to observable order in creation as evidence of divine justice. From this angle, suffering is often interpreted as a moral consequence woven

---

[9] Cf. Barry D. Smith, "Suffering," in *Evangelical Dictionary of Biblical Theology*, eds. Walter A. Elwell and Walter A. Elwell, electronic ed., Baker reference library; Logos Library System (Grand Rapids: Baker Book House, 1997).

into the fabric of the universe itself—a reflection of a moral structure that governs both heaven and earth.[10]

The understanding of suffering in the Ancient Near East and early religious worldview often included the belief that the displeasure of gods, demons, or evil spirits could cause misfortune. When individuals or communities experienced suffering, it was frequently interpreted as the result of supernatural beings expressing their anger or disappointment. At the core of this worldview was a strong belief in retribution or recompense theology, a moral framework rooted in the principle of sowing and reaping.[11]

This concept is clearly reflected in the Mosaic Covenant, where obedience to God's commands results in blessing, while disobedience brings about divine curses. According to this theological structure, the outcome of a person's life, whether marked by peace or affliction, was directly linked to their moral behaviour. Throughout the history of Israel, there have been many occasions where the nation justly

---

[10] Cf. Greg W. Parsons, "Guidelines for understanding and Proclaiming the Book of Job," in *Bibliotheca Sacra* 15 (October-December 1994): 403.

[11] Cf. Larry J. Waters, "Reflections on Suffering from the Book of Job," *Bibliotheca Sacra* 154 (October–December 1997): 3.

deserved divine judgment because of its rebellion and wickedness. However, even in those moments, the grace of God was evident. Rather than responding solely with punishment, God often chose to show mercy, revealing His long-suffering character and unwavering commitment to His covenant promises despite the people's repeated failures.[12]

This view raises serious challenges and is increasingly questioned, both theologically and philosophically. First, it risks oversimplifying the complex nature of suffering by reducing it to a matter of cause and effect based purely on moral outcomes. Human experience and Scripture alike show that suffering can occur independently of personal sin or wrongdoing. Innocent people suffer, and misfortune often strikes without a clear moral cause or explanation. This reality undermines the assumption that all suffering is just punishment or inherited guilt.

The ancient worldview that attributes suffering to the displeasure of gods or spiritual beings reflects a more mythological understanding. The understanding of suffering has not remained static but has developed progressively over

---

[12] Ibid., 3.

time, a process of evolving reflection that can be clearly observed throughout the Hebrew Scriptures. As the experiences of individuals and the nation of Israel unfolded, so too did their interpretation of suffering, deepening from a simple cause-and-effect model into a more complex theological and existential inquiry.

1.2.2 Pre-exilic Perspective

According to the pre-exilic worldview, suffering is closely tied to human disobedience, a theme that emerges clearly in the early chapters of Genesis, particularly chapters two and three. According to the biblical explanation of origins, the narrative of the fall provides the foundational explanation for the presence of suffering in the world. Genesis chapter three presents a vivid portrayal of how suffering entered the human story, not as a result of divine cruelty or negligence, but through the deliberate choice to disobey God's clear command.[13]

Humanity, created in a state of goodness and life without pain or death, was given the gift of free will. In choosing to

---

[13] Cf. Daniel J. Simundson, "Suffering," in *The Anchor Yale Bible Dictionary,* ed. David Noel Freedman, vol. 6 (New York: Doubleday, 1996), 220.

test the boundaries of God's instruction, the first man and woman brought upon themselves the consequences of separation, toil, pain, and mortality. The account does not question the goodness, omniscience, or love of God. Instead, it affirms God's moral integrity while placing the weight of responsibility upon human decision. Biblical theology maintains this view by affirming that God's nature remains just and loving, even as humanity bears the consequences of its rebellion. According to this pre-exilic interpretation, the entrance of suffering into the world is the result of a moral fall, not divine failure. The pain and disorder experienced in creation trace back to the original disobedience, through which all of humanity has inherited a condition of vulnerability and brokenness.[14]

1.2.3 Deuteronomistic History

The book of Deuteronomy presents a covenantal framework in which obedience to God's law results in blessings, while disobedience leads to curses. This theological structure is central to what scholars refer to as the Deuteronomistic History, a perspective that runs through much of Israel's

---

[14] Ibid.

narrative from Deuteronomy through Kings. Deuteronomy chapters 27 and 28 clearly outline the expected moral behaviour of God's people, setting before them both the rewards of faithfulness and the consequences of rebellion. These passages show that suffering is not random, but is the just outcome of turning away from divine instruction. Within this framework, one might even understand the reasoning of Job's friends, who assumed that Job's suffering, particularly the affliction of painful boils, could be evidence of unfaithfulness, perhaps drawing from the warnings in Deuteronomy 28:35. However, the climax of the book offers a profound choice.[15]

In Deuteronomy 30:15-20, God places before His people the decision between life and death, between good and evil. This crucial moment reveals the moral foundation upon which human suffering is often understood in Hebrew Scriptures. It emphasises human responsibility and the real consequences of moral choice, while also reflecting the covenantal nature of God's relationship with His people. Suffering, from this view, is not without cause or meaning, but is deeply tied to the ethical and spiritual choices humanity makes before God.

---

[15] Ibid.

In the book of Joshua, the narrative presents a striking example of how the sin of a single individual can bring suffering upon an entire community. This principle, resembling the ripple effect, is vividly illustrated in the story of Achan found in chapter seven. After the conquest of Jericho, Achan disobeyed God's command by secretly taking for himself items that had been set apart for destruction. As a result of his hidden transgression, the Israelites were unexpectedly defeated in their next battle at Ai. This defeat was not only a military setback but also a spiritual crisis that revealed the serious consequences of covenant violation. When Achan's guilt was exposed, divine judgment fell not only upon him but also upon his entire household, highlighting the communal impact of an individual sin. This account suggests that suffering is not always the result of one's own wrongdoing.[16]

Sometimes, the pain endured by the innocent is the consequence of another's rebellion against God. It highlights a central theme within the Deuteronomistic tradition: human sin, whether personal or collective, disrupts the covenantal relationship with God and invites suffering into the broader

---

[16] Ibid.

community. In this view, suffering is not random but is often the outworking of moral failure that affects others far beyond the initial act of disobedience.[17]

It is possible that Job's understanding of suffering and the tragic loss of his children was shaped by a worldview similar to that found in the Deuteronomistic tradition, where the sin of one can bring consequences upon others. In Job 1:5, we see him regularly offering burnt sacrifices on behalf of his children, fearing that in the midst of their feasting, they may have sinned or inwardly cursed God.

This practice suggests that Job was deeply aware of the potential for hidden sin to provoke divine judgment, not only upon the sinner but also upon those closely connected to them. Job's actions reflect a deep sense of moral responsibility and a desire to intercede, even proactively, on behalf of his family, revealing how seriously he regarded the possibility that suffering could be the result of unacknowledged or unintentional offence against God.

The theme of retributive justice is evident throughout the narrative of Judges. This book presents a cyclical pattern in

---

[17] Ibid.

which the fate of the Israelites, whether marked by victory or defeat, depends on their response to God's covenant. When the people remained faithful to God's commands, they experienced peace, stability, and divine favour. However, when they turned away in disobedience and followed other gods, they suffered oppression, defeat, and turmoil. This recurring pattern reveals that their future was not random but was directly shaped by the moral and spiritual choices they made.[18]

The message from the book of Judges highlights the serious weight of human freedom, showing that the blessings or sufferings experienced by the nation were not merely circumstantial but deeply tied to their covenantal faithfulness. At the heart of the narrative is the affirmation that God acts justly, responding to both obedience and rebellion with appropriate consequence. Thus, the book of Judges teaches that suffering often arises as the outcome of wrong choices, and it serves as a theological reminder of the cost of forsaking God's ways.

---

[18] Ibid.

Conclusion

The question of suffering touches the deepest parts of human existence and calls for thoughtful theological reflection. From a secular viewpoint, suffering is often understood as a natural and unavoidable reality arising from the complexities of life and human limitations. This perspective emphasises human responsibility, compassion, and the pursuit of happiness as ways to confront pain in a world without divine intervention.

In contrast, the Hebrew perspective roots suffering in the moral and spiritual order established by God. It sees suffering as a consequence of human disobedience and the fracture of the relationship between Creator and creation. The biblical narrative reveals that suffering entered the world not through God's will but through the misuse of human freedom. The covenantal framework found throughout the Hebrew Scriptures highlights how obedience leads to blessing and disobedience brings hardship, affirming that suffering carries meaning within God's just governance.

Throughout the ancient texts, suffering is understood as both personal and communal, often affecting entire communities because of individual or collective sin. Theologically, suffering cannot be dismissed as meaningless or merely accidental. It reveals the brokenness of a world that longs for redemption, and calls forth a response grounded in faith, repentance, and trust in God's promise of restoration.

Job challenges the theological assumptions found in the Deuteronomistic tradition. If suffering is always a sign of divine punishment for sin, then Job should be an exception that breaks the rule. Yet his story refuses to fit into the neat categories of retribution theology, exposing the limitations of human reasoning about God's justice and forcing a deeper encounter with divine mystery. With this understanding, the book now turns to the Old Testament, where ancient perspectives on affliction, justice, and divine providence take shape, leading to the profound and challenging story of Job.

Chapter Two:
The Nature and Causes of Suffering: The Book of Job as a Lens on Suffering

Within the breadth of Scripture, two books stand out for their profound and unflinching engagement with the reality of suffering: the book of Job and the book of Lamentations, alongside the passion narratives in the Gospels. Lamentations presents a collective lament, expressing the grief and devastation of Israel after the fall of Jerusalem, while Job offers a more personal and philosophical exploration of suffering through the experience of a single righteous man. Through intense dialogue with his friends, the narrative probes the heart of theodicy and challenges readers to confront suffering without easy answers.

Often considered one of the earliest written books in the biblical canon, Job reflects ancient Near Eastern understandings of suffering and wrestles with retribution theology, the belief that suffering is directly tied to wrongdoing. The friends' responses are rooted in this worldview, which seeks to interpret suffering as divine recompense. Yet Job's story refuses to fit neatly into this framework. Rather than offering simplistic explanations, the book invites readers into a profound journey of faith where human wisdom reaches its limits and divine encounter becomes necessary.

Job holds a unique place within the canon because it is both poetic and dramatic, and because it does not centre on covenantal law or ritual worship. The protagonist appears outside the typical Israelite religious framework, allowing the book to address universal questions of suffering, righteousness, and divine sovereignty beyond ethnic boundaries. The Hebrew language, with its symbolic imagery and layered meaning, further deepens the narrative and encourages the reader to look beneath the surface for the deeper truths the author intends to communicate.

The opening chapters, particularly Job 1:6–12 and 2:1–7, raise a critical question: Is suffering ultimately from God, from Satan, or the result of personal or communal sin? A literal reading of the divine dialogue can mislead readers into thinking God directly wills Job's suffering, but this is only one possible interpretation. To understand the passage fully, we must read it within its literary and cultural context and through a Hebraic lens. As a result, Job offers several perspectives on suffering, evil, purification, mystery, and providence, without resolving the question in a way that satisfies human reasoning.

2.1 Retribution Theory

The principle of sowing and reaping, often referred to as retribution or recompense theology, is a concept found throughout both the Old Testament and the New Testament. Passages such as Matthew 16:27, Romans 2:6, 2 Corinthians 5:10, Galatians 6:7, Revelation 2:23, and 20:13 in the New Testament, along with Job 4:8, Proverbs 22:8, Jeremiah 17:10, 32:19, and Ezekiel 18:20 in the Hebrew Scriptures, affirm that individuals reap what they sow, meaning that one's actions directly lead to corresponding consequences.

This idea carries a universal appeal and has been accepted as a general truth by many throughout biblical history. However, this belief encounters difficulty when confronted with the suffering of innocent individuals. The book of Job does not provide a straightforward explanation for why Job suffers; rather, it explores various explanations, including those from Ancient Near Eastern thought, that attempt to give meaning and hope in the midst of suffering.

Job's friends, drawing on retributive theology, insist that Job's suffering must be the result of sin or wrongdoing. Zophar, for example, declares in chapter 20 that the wicked will inevitably suffer for their misdeeds. Bildad similarly emphasises God's punishment upon the wicked in chapter 18, implying Job's affliction is deserved.

Eliphaz echoes this in his speeches, accusing Job of hidden sins (4-5, 22:5). Yet, this retribution view contradicts the opening portrayal of Job as blameless and upright (1:1) and is ultimately challenged by God's declaration in 42:7, showing that suffering is not always the result of personal sin. Thus, while the principle of retribution offers an initial framework, it fails to fully account for the complex reality of innocent suffering depicted in the book of Job.

2.2 Wager Theory

One of the causes of Job's suffering is attributed to the wager between God and Satan, where Job's faith and integrity are tested through divine permission for Satan to bring trials upon him.[19]

Dr. Bernard Leikind, a physicist, observes the divine engagement with the profound test of human suffering. He suggests that, in a way, God appears to accept a challenge posed by Satan. A challenge that puts the faithfulness of Job under intense trial. The terms are clear and uncompromising: if Job, faced with unimaginable pain and loss, reacts by renouncing or cursing God, then Satan's wager is won. On the other hand, if Job remains steadfast, refusing to abandon his trust in God despite his suffering, then God emerges victorious in this contest. This analogy draws attention to the mysterious interplay between divine sovereignty and human free will in the face of evil. Leikind questions the wisdom of engaging in such a gamble, especially when one considers that God, as omniscient, would have full knowledge of the outcome. [20]

---

[19] Cf. William David Reyburn, A *Handbook on the Book of Job* (New York: United Bible Societies, 1992), 8.

[20] Cf. Bernard Leikind, "The Mystery of Evil and Suffering," *TheHumanist.com*, accessed May 29, 2018, http://thehumanist.com/magazine/may-june-2010/commentary/the-mystery-of-evil-and-suffering.

However, John E. Hartley challenges the common interpretation of the wager theory in this context, arguing that it falls short of making sense because there is no tangible reward or prize promised to the victor. While many scholars have understood the dialogue between God and Satan as a form of wager, Hartley observes that the lack of any clear reward or restitution makes it harder to accept this view. His insight invites readers to reconsider the nature of this divine exchange, encouraging a deeper exploration of the purpose and meaning behind the trials of Job beyond mere contest or gamble.[21]

While cancelling the wager theory, the author of Job reveals a worldview deeply rooted in the Ancient Near Eastern understanding of God as the ultimate sovereign, fully responsible for all occurrences, whether cosmic, physical, natural, or spiritual. This perspective highlights the comprehensive authority of God over every dimension of existence, affirming that nothing happens outside of His divine governance and purpose.[22]

---

[21] Cf. John E. Hartley, *The Book of Job* (Grand Rapids: Wm. B. Eerdmans Publishing Co., 1988), 74.

[22] Ibid. Also see: Job 2:3; Is 45:7.

In the Old Testament, God, referred to as *Yahweh*, is portrayed as the source of all things, including both good and evil. Early Hebrew belief did not distinguish between positive and negative experiences as separate from God's will. Everything that happened, whether it brought joy or suffering, was seen as coming directly from God. Because of this, the concept of evil was not seen as a problem or contradiction for the ancient Hebrews. They accepted that misfortune and blessings alike were expressions of divine power. However, as their moral understanding became more developed over time, the Hebrews began to feel unsettled by the idea of a God who could cause both harm and good without apparent reason. [23]

2.3 Does God Cause Suffering?

Isaiah 45:7 offers a profound glimpse into the Ancient Near Eastern worldview that shapes the theology of Job's friends, who interpret his misfortunes as divinely appointed events intended to reveal God's hidden purpose through suffering. The verse, "I form the light and create darkness, I make peace and create calamity; I, the LORD, do all these things,"

---

[23] Cf. Richard Rohr, *Job and the Mystery of Suffering: Spiritual Reflection,* 45.

serves as a foundational text for understanding divine sovereignty in the book of Job. However, it raises a challenging theological question: Is God the creator of evil?

The Hebrew verb ברא (*bara*)[24], meaning "to create," and the noun רַע (*rah*), often translated as "evil" or "calamity," together suggest that God has authority not only over peace and light but also over darkness and disaster. This pairing can lead to the troubling impression that God is the source of moral evil, a conclusion that demands careful hermeneutical discernment.[25]

---

[24] ברא is used only to God for His creative principle. In this verb only God is the subject. Cf. Warren Baker, "ברא" in *The Complete Word Study Dictionary: Old Testament* (Chattanooga, TN: AMG Publishers, 2003), 161.

[25] To understand this passage, one must know the entire context of the chapter and have an understanding of Second Isaiah. This passage is written in the context of the Israelites in exile, where God uses Cyrus as His instrument. As a poetic passage, it addresses the Zoroastrian concept of dualism, which was a religion in Persia during the time of Cyrus. According to Zoroastrianism, there are two gods or forces in heaven that are equally powerful. Ahura Mazda is the creator of light and peace, and Angra Mainyu is the creator of darkness and evil. Hence, in order to counter this belief in dualism in light of monotheism, the highlight of this passage is "I, the LORD, do all these things," meaning that God is in control whether during times of peace or times of evil. Cf. David Guzik, *The Enduring Word Commentary Series (Isa–Mal)*, electronic ed., Is. 45:4–7.

For those who interpret God's role in Job 1:12 and 2:6 as that of the ultimate cause behind all human events, it appears justified that God permitted Satan to afflict Job, since nothing occurs apart from divine permission. From this perspective, God becomes the one who allowed the death of Job's children and the destruction of his possessions, not as a passive observer, but as the one who sanctioned the test. Such a view risks portraying God as harsh or even sadistic, willingly subjecting a righteous man to profound suffering for the sake of a heavenly contest. This interpretation is reinforced in Job 2:10, where Job himself declares that both good and evil come from God, underscoring the belief that divine providence encompasses all dimensions of human experience.

Within this framework, God is not only sovereign over blessings but also over pain and loss. Eliphaz, reflecting this worldview, sees God as both the source and the solution to suffering. Eliphaz assumes that Job's afflictions must be punishment for hidden sin and that restoration is possible if

Job repents.[26] According to Eliphaz, mercy and the intervention of God are given selectively. Therefore, Eliphaz argues that it calls for סָכַן (*cakan or saw-kan*), a surrendering or coming to terms with and שׁוּב (*Shuwb*), meaning to turn back to God – repent.[27]

If God is truly all-powerful, all-knowing, ever-present, and all-loving, then the question arises: why does He permit the existence of evil? In Job 1:10, a profound scene unfolds between God and Satan, where God draws attention to Job as a man of integrity and uprightness who fears God and turns from evil. Satan, however, challenges the sincerity of Job's devotion, suggesting that his faithfulness is not born out of genuine reverence but is merely a response to divine protection and prosperity.

Satan implies that if God were to remove His blessings, Job would curse Him openly. In response, God grants Satan permission to test Job, placing all he possesses under Satan's

---

[26] Eliphaz's perspective of God as the originator and reliever of suffering is based on retribution theology – Eliphaz mentions Job's past sin is the reason of Job's plight. See. Job 15:5-6, 20; 22:5-11.

[27] סָכַן (*cakan or saw-kan'*) means to be useful, however based on the given context סָכַן also means "come to terms with" in 22:21. Cf. Stephen M. Hooks, *Job* (Joplin: College Press Pub., 2006), 282.

control, but forbidding him from harming Job himself (1:12). This passage promotes God as one who allows evil.

In early Hebraic thought, God was understood as the ultimate initiator of all things, both blessing and calamity, with no need to separate divine causality into categories of good and evil. Suffering was not perceived as incompatible with God's nature, but rather as something within His sovereign domain. This is evident in passages such as Amos 3:6, which affirms that no disaster befalls a city unless the Lord has acted, and in the book of Exodus, where God is said to have hardened Pharaoh's heart. Such texts reflect a worldview in which God's authority encompasses the entire spectrum of human experience, including hardships.

This perception persisted well into Christian thought, where many continued to hold that God could use even suffering or moral resistance to bring about His greater purposes and manifest His glory. However, as theology progressed, the understanding of God and His character began to take shape.[28]

---

[28] Richard Rohr, *Job and the Mystery of Suffering: Spiritual Reflection*, 37.

While Scripture contains passages that indicate the duality of God as the source of both blessing and calamity,[29] Job himself never embraced the notion that God would allow innocent suffering without just cause. Although Job openly acknowledges that he is not without sin, he remains firmly convinced that he has not committed any wrongdoing deserving of the intense affliction he endures, a conviction grounded deeply in his personal relationship with God.

On the other hand, Job's friends seek to comfort him by urging him to accept his suffering as a form of divine discipline or judgment, while it is clear from the Book of Job and other supporting Scriptures that, as an innocent man, Job's suffering does not originate from God.

---

[29] The idea of duality in God appears in the Book of Job and other writings. For the Israelites of the pre-exilic era, pain was not seen as a separate mystery. They understood God to be present in all events, both good and bad. Unlike neighboring religions, which assigned different aspects of life to multiple gods, the Israelites embraced monotheism, seeing one God as sovereign over everything. Their explanations of suffering were often simple, reflecting their developing understanding of God and the limits of their knowledge. From the Hebraic perspective, every event in the world ultimately reveals God's righteousness. Cf. James Strahan, *The Book of Job Interpreted* (Edinburgh: T. & T. Clark, 1913), 4–5, 75. However, in the book of Job, we see a new perspective on suffering, as Job questions centuries old tradition of duality of God, to which he refutes by defending and bringing a different kind of understanding of God.

2.4 Can Suffering Serve as Correction?

Elihu suggests that suffering can serve as God's instrument for correction, as noted in Job 33:19, and that it acts to keep people from destruction, according to Job 33:29-30, while also bringing about a deep inner awareness of God's presence, as described in Job 37:24. For Elihu, suffering is not ultimately destructive for those whom God uses it to mature spiritually; rather, it is a purposeful tool employed to establish a person's life in greater maturity and to deepen their faith despite human weakness.[30]

Additionally, Elihu introduces the concept of divine retribution, emphasising that suffering can be a just response to human behaviour, strengthening the moral order while simultaneously serving as a means of growth and restoration. Robert Alden acknowledges that the principle itself is fundamentally sound and consistently affirmed throughout Scripture. However, he critiques the way Job's four friends rigidly apply this principle to Job's situation. Their approach

---

[30] Cf. *The Essence of the Old Testament*, eds. Edward Hindson and Gary Yates (Nashville: B&H Academic, 2012), 245.

fails to consider future divine justice and shows no compassion or mercy toward Job's suffering.[31]

David Sper understands suffering as a purposeful instrument to alert us, direct us, shape us, and unite us. His view on suffering is not merely as a negative experience but as a meaningful instrument in God's hands.[32] The idea that suffering serves as a means of correction and spiritual discipline from God is a widely held conviction throughout Christian tradition. A book released by the United Church of God states,

> God sometimes allows such discomfort—and suffering—to cause us to pay attention to what we are doing and change our behavior, attitude or convictions...In allowing discomfort to bring mistakes and character flaws to our attention, God is no different from any other loving parent. Fathers and mothers who love their children invest time and effort teaching and enforcing lessons for their good. God does the same because He wants us to learn (Hebrews 12:5-11). God sometimes allows us to suffer so we will learn right from wrong and will realise our dependence on Him and His instruction. Therefore we should not be surprised when life,

---

[31] Cf. Robert L. Alden, "Job," in *The New American Commentary*, vol. 11 (Nashville: Broadman & Holman Publishers, 2001), 335.

[32] Cf. David Sper, *Why Would a Good God Allow Suffering* (Grand Rapids: RBC Ministries, 2001), 1.

even for a Christian, includes stress and trials (1 Peter 4:12-13).[33]

In the quoted passage, the depiction of God as a disciplining parent is supported by Hebrews 12:5-11. Although such an anthropomorphic portrayal may not fully capture the infinite and transcendent nature of God, it provides a relatable framework for human beings to understand and connect with the divine. By referencing this Scripture, the danger is that suffering is a form of divine discipline or chastening. However, this interpretation is based on a simplistic and flawed interpretation that ignores context and nuance, overlooking the profound complexity and richness of the Scripture.

The central term in Hebrews 12:5-11 is παιδεία (*paideia*), often translated as chastening or discipline. The most widespread interpretation suggests that God uses suffering as a means to discipline His people. Suffering typically carries a negative implication, which can conflict with the fuller meaning of παιδεία (*paideia*). It is understood as instruction through action, correction, and a form of educative discipline. This concept of παιδεία (*paideia*) contrasts sharply with terms like

---

[33] *Why Does God Allow Suffering?* (Ohio: United Church of God, 2008), 25.

κόλασις (*kólasis*), meaning penal retribution, and τιμωρία (*timōría*), which refers to penalty or punishment, both emphasising punitive consequences.[34]

Therefore, reading suffering into this passage as simply a tool of divine punishment risks imposing an eisegetical distortion that unfairly casts God's character in a harsh light and misrepresents the nature of Job's suffering.

Moreover, Rohr states, "God can set us right only by breaking us down… We're going to see in Job how God breaks this man down so he can enter into a newer and better definition of truth, a better understanding of how God creates life on earth."[35]

Rohr holds the view that within the mysterious framework of God's sovereign goodness and divine order, evil and affliction are not outside His purposes but can be employed as instruments through which God works to accomplish deeper spiritual ends. He suggests that God, in His wisdom, may permit or use experiences of suffering and moral evil not as

---

[34] Spiros Zodhiates, "παιδεία," in *The Complete Word Study Dictionary: New Testament*, electronic ed. (Chattanooga, TN: AMG Publishers, 2000), G3809.

[35] Richard Rohr, *Job and the Mystery of Suffering: Spiritual Reflection*, 44.

ends in themselves, but as means through which the human heart is awakened, refined, and drawn into closer communion with the Divine.[36]

If the conclusion drawn by the Joban author, that every human event, whether good or evil, proceeds from God, is to be accepted uncritically, it presents a contradiction to the broader witness of Scripture. However, the unity of its subject matter is ultimately preserved in its conclusion, where Elihu challenges Job's earlier assertion in 9:20-24 by affirming in 37:23 that God does not oppress.[37] Therefore, Richard's interpretation that God employs evil to bring humanity closer to Himself deserves serious critique, since it can lead to a distorted picture of God that does not align with Scripture as a whole.

Although the worldview of the Ancient Near East often attributes all cosmic and human events directly to God as part of His sovereign relationship with creation, Elihu in the

---

[36] Ibid.

[37] Cf. Marvin H. Pope, "Job," in *The Anchor Yale Bible Commentary*, vol. 15 (London: Yale University Press, 2008), 287. The Hebrew word used for oppress is עָנָה (ʿanah) meaning to afflict or inflict oppression. Cf. Warren Baker, "עָנָה," in The Complete Word Study Dictionary: Old Testament (Chattanooga, TN: AMG Publishers, 2003), 852.

Book of Job clearly challenges this understanding. Elihu denies that God is the direct cause of every human experience, including good, evil, or suffering, thereby rejecting the idea that God unreasonably ordains all such events. This distinction marks a critical departure within the text, emphasising that not all occurrences, especially suffering, can be attributed to God's direct causation.[38]

---

[38] According to many scholars, the structure, theology, and the distinct section devoted to Elihu's speeches suggest that these chapters are later additions to the Book of Job. However, recent research challenges this perspective. See Cf. Patricia A. MacNicoll, "Elihu," in *Eerdmans Dictionary of the Bible*, eds. David Noel Freedman, Allen C. Myers and Astrid B. Beck (Grand Rapids: W.B. Eerdmans, 2000), 395. Also see, J. Gerald Janzen, *Job, Interpretation, A Bible Commentary for Teaching and Preaching* (Atlanta: John Knox Press, 1985), 217.

Conclusion

The Book of Job explores the mystery of human suffering from multiple angles. Job's friends argue from the retribution theory, insisting that suffering is a sign of sin, but Job's blamelessness challenges this logic. The wager between God and Satan introduces trials, yet its purpose and fairness remain debated, highlighting tension between divine sovereignty and human experience. Passages like Isaiah 45:7 portray God as sovereign over both blessings and calamities, complicating traditional notions of good and evil. Elihu presents suffering as corrective, guiding moral and spiritual growth, but he carefully separates this from the direct cause of evil.

Together, these perspectives illustrate that suffering cannot be fully understood by human reasoning alone, pointing instead to the mystery of God's wisdom and the limits of human comprehension.

The next chapter will turn to God's response in the divine speeches, exploring how God answers Job's questions and what that reveals about the nature of suffering, justice, and divine presence.

Chapter Three:
Christian Responses to Suffering, in Conversation with Job

This chapter will explore how Job shapes Christian responses to suffering, and what it means to hold faith in God without easy answers.

There are many different views within Christianity about suffering, and these depend on how people interpret the Bible. The book of Job is often used to help understand what suffering means. Pain and suffering cannot be fully understood by study alone; they are harsh realities of life that can only be truly grasped through the grace of God. Many Christians believe that God uses suffering as a tool to test and strengthen the faith of His people.

Even though the story of Job shows God's silence in suffering, and this remains a mystery, people still try to find meaning in pain. God is present not only in our happiness and conscience but also in our pain, says C. S. Lewis. To revive this deaf world, pain is His megaphone. This means that God uses suffering to get our attention and bring us closer to Him, even when it is difficult to understand, according to Lewis.[39]

3.1 Suffering as an Instrument

Many Christians believe suffering is tied to the freedom God gave us. We were made with the ability to choose, and that includes the ability to turn away from God. When people use their freedom wrongly, it causes a lot of the pain and brokenness we see in the world. Even so, suffering still feels mysterious. It can be crushing, confusing, and unfair. But for many believers, it is not something God ignores. Instead, they trust that even when we don't understand, God is still present and working in the midst of it.

That does not mean suffering is good or that we should accept it easily. It simply means that, rather than demanding answers, many Christians try to respond with trust and humility. They believe that God's wisdom is greater than ours, and that suffering can become a place where faith is tested, shaped, and deepened.

---

[39] Cf. C. S. Lewis, *The Problem of Pain* (New York: Macmillan Publishing Co., 1978), 93.

However, Job's story complicates Lewis' picture because Job was already faithful before his suffering began. This challenges the idea that suffering is always a punishment or a lesson for wrongdoing. Sometimes it simply happens to good people, and that is one of the hardest truths to hold.

C. S. Lewis presents pain as a divine instrument, a kind of spiritual compass, that alerts individuals when they are drifting away from the path of truth and righteousness. In his view, pain is not merely a disruption to human comfort but a meaningful opportunity for reflection, repentance, and realignment with the will of God. It serves as a grace-filled interruption, prompting the human heart to reconsider its course and to become open to the goodness and mercy of God. Lewis suggests that a life marked only by comfort, sufficiency, and superficial happiness often lacks a true awareness of God, as such a life leaves little room for dependence on anything beyond the self.

When this false sense of happiness eventually disappears, as it surely will, pain exposes the emptiness it leaves behind and draws the soul into a state of surrender. Therefore, pain becomes a paradoxical gift, breaking the illusion of self-sufficiency and guiding the soul toward true transformation and union with God.[40]

While there is some truth in Lewis's idea of placing God through suffering, his portrayal risks making God seem almost childish, as if He uses pain simply to catch our attention. This understanding does not fit well with the story of Job, who was already deeply mindful of God before his suffering began, as seen in Job 1:5. It would be unfair and theologically inaccurate to suggest that God deliberately inflicts pain to draw His people's notice. Instead, pain and suffering, though not essential, can serve as one of the ways through which a person's focus is drawn toward God. The Christian life calls us to look beyond the pain to Jesus, described in Hebrews 12:2 as the author and perfecter of our faith.

In seeking to understand suffering, some have believed that discovering its meaning or purpose might ease the burden of pain. A common perspective is that suffering functions as a form of testing, measuring a person's endurance and resilience. Those who persevere through hardship are

---

[40] Ibid., 95-96.

thought to emerge with greater strength or moral stature, while those who struggle are often encouraged to reflect on their lives and discern areas of weakness or failure. In this view, suffering becomes an opportunity for personal growth and spiritual refinement, offering the chance to correct past mistakes and deepen one's dependence on God.[41]

3.2 Suffering and the Glory of God

In his book, Christopher Ash argues that the suffering experienced by Job, though inflicted by Satan, serves a higher and necessary purpose; namely, the glory of God. Even if Ash's intention is to uphold God's glory, the language may unintentionally suggest a distant God.

Job's suffering is not presented as random or as the result of a careless wager between God and Satan. Instead, it is shown as something God allows in order to reveal the genuineness of faith. As Job remains faithful despite loss and pain, the story makes clear that God is not worthy of worship merely because He gives blessings, but because of who He is. Satan's role is that of an accuser, not a rival equal to God, and his

---

[41] Cf. John L. Yardan, *God and the Challenge of Evil* (USA: LCCiP, 2001), 163-164.

actions unfold within God's sovereign purposes. Job's trials, therefore, serve a greater end: they bear witness to authentic faith and point to the magnification of God's name, even when God's purposes remain beyond human understanding.[42] Ash continues to write, "If the Satan did not issue this challenge, it would be necessary for God to delegate this terrible task to another supernatural creature."[43]

Ash argues that Job's suffering, though inflicted by Satan, ultimately serves God's glory. While Ash likely intends to uphold God's sovereignty, the word 'necessary' can unintentionally be heard as implying that God needs suffering for His glory. This can be difficult for sufferers to hear, especially when they need comfort more than explanation. A more careful wording would affirm God's sovereignty without implying that innocent suffering is required for God to be glorified.

Furthermore, Scripture affirms that God's glory is most fully revealed not through the suffering of the innocent as a

---

[42] Cf. Christopher Ash, *Job The Wisdom of the Cross*, ed. R. Kent Hughes (Illinois: Crossway, 2014), 44–45.
[43] Ibid., 45.

dramatic show, but through the redemptive suffering of Christ, who willingly took on suffering not to prove a point, but to redeem and reconcile. Job's suffering, while mysterious, cannot be reduced to a divine experiment to validate faith. As Job himself insists throughout the book, he is not suffering as a means to display his loyalty or God's worth, but is caught in the uncertainty of righteous suffering that remains unexplained. This mystery of suffering is not resolved by a theological explanation, but by an encounter with the living God.

While Ash seeks to uphold the glory of God, the language of necessity raises a serious pastoral concern. If suffering is presented as something God needs in order to receive worship, it can be difficult for those who are hurting to hear. Many people who suffer deeply do not need theological arguments; they need compassion, comfort, and the assurance that God is near.

When suffering is framed as a necessary means to an end, it can unintentionally make God sound distant or uncaring. That kind of picture can drive people away from faith rather than draw them closer to it. The God revealed in Jesus Christ is one who brings glory through love, not through manipulation, and who walks with the suffering rather than using their pain as a tool for a greater purpose.

Moreover, Ash draws a theological connection between the message of the Petrine epistle and the narrative of Job to offer a deeper understanding of suffering, particularly that which befalls the righteous. By referencing 1 Peter 1:7, which speaks of the trials that test the genuineness of faith and result in praise, honour, and glory, Ash frames the suffering of Job within the broader biblical narrative of redemptive testing. The implication is that suffering, especially when endured by the innocent, is not meaningless but is allowed by God for a higher purpose. It becomes a means through which faith is refined, and God's glory is ultimately revealed. According to Ash, Job's affliction serves not only as a personal trial but also as a divine demonstration of authentic faith, echoing the apostolic affirmation that suffering has eternal significance when it reveals the endurance and purity of belief. This theological alignment presents suffering not merely as a burden to bear, but as an occasion for divine validation and eschatological reward.[44]

---

[44] Ibid.

It is theologically possible to say that suffering may ultimately bring glory to God. However, Ash's claim that suffering is "necessary" for that purpose must be treated with caution. If God is understood to intentionally orchestrate suffering to prove faith or secure worship, the result can be a picture of God that feels cold, distant, or even cruel. Many people who have suffered deeply do not need theology; they need mercy. To suggest that their pain is required for God's glory can unintentionally make God appear indifferent to human suffering.

This is why the language matters. If God is seen as using suffering as a tool, it can lead to the belief that God is more interested in His own praise than in the well-being of His people. In the minds of those who suffer, this can begin to sound like a God who is a sadist, taking pleasure in pain, or a narcissist, primarily preoccupied with preserving His own glory. Such an impression conflicts with the God revealed in Scripture as compassionate, merciful, and close to the brokenhearted.

While Ash's connection between Job's suffering and the trials mentioned in 1 Peter 1:7 aims to place suffering within a redemptive narrative, it risks conflating two distinct theological contexts. The Petrine epistle speaks to believers who suffer because of their allegiance to Christ, highlighting eschatological hope and the purification of faith in the face of persecution. Job's story, however, belongs to a different covenant and a different narrative purpose. It does not specifically point to messianic suffering or suffering for redemption.

Job is not portrayed as a sufferer for righteousness in a missional or gospel-proclaiming sense, but rather as a blameless man caught in a cosmic dispute between God and Satan. His experience is a personal and unique struggle with the mystery of suffering, God's silence, and the search for justice. Therefore, applying the Petrine framework to Job risks overlooking the distinctiveness of his story and the specific questions it raises about innocent suffering.

Drawing a direct connection between the suffering described in 1 Peter and the suffering of Job is not straightforward. In 1 Peter 1:6, the verse says that believers may be "grieved by various trials, if necessary." The Greek phrase behind "if necessary" does not mean that suffering is always required. Instead, it suggests that suffering may happen when God allows it for a purpose. This makes it hard to apply the same idea to Job. Peter is addressing Christians who are being persecuted because of their faith. Job, however, is not suffering as a result of persecution or for the sake of the gospel. His suffering comes from a very different situation, and the book of Job explores a different kind of mystery.[45]

Allen Black and Mark C. Black argue that suffering can serve as a necessary test to prove the genuineness of faith, which is described as more precious than gold (1 Peter 1:7). They see suffering—often caused by evil people—as part of God's plan to refine believers.[46] However, John H. Elliott challenges this view by pointing to the conditional wording in 1 Peter 1:6. The verse says believers may be "grieved by various trials, if necessary," suggesting that suffering is not always required but may occur when God allows it for a purpose.[47]

This distinction matters because it prevents the idea that all Christians must suffer as a test of faith. Similar language

---

[45] Cf. Pheme Perkins, *First and Second Peter, James, and Jude, Interpretation, a Bible Commentary for Teaching and Preaching* (Louisville: John Knox Press, 1995), 30.

[46] Cf. Allen Black and Mark C. Black, *1 & 2 Peter, The College Press NIV Commentary* (Joplin: College Press Pub., 1998), 1 Pe 1:6.

[47] Cf. John H. Elliott, *1 Peter: A New Translation with Introduction and Commentary* (New Haven; London: Yale University Press, 2008), 340.

appears in 1 Peter 3:14 and 3:17, reinforcing that suffering happens only when it is necessary, not as a universal mandate. Therefore, we should be careful not to treat suffering as an automatic requirement in God's plan.

3.3 A Christian Response to Suffering: Insights from the Book of Job

The key message is that God remains in control, not as the one who causes evil, but as the one who is present and faithful during times of suffering.

The writer of Job presents an innocent man who endures great pain and suffering. Because of this, many Christians turn to the book of Job to understand their own suffering. The common belief among Christians is similar to what Job's friends said: suffering happens because of sin, whether it is known or unknown, in the family, or because someone has not followed God or repented.

Many people find it hard to deal with suffering. It can make them feel guilty or blame themselves. Suffering can either help a person grow and become stronger in facing challenges, or it can make them bitter and broken. The book of Job shows us how suffering is complicated and reminds us that in the middle of pain, we need God.

The New Testament often focus on suffering related to persecution. Because of this, it is important to be cautious when applying these texts to other kinds of suffering. The story of Job, who suffers without any known reason even though he is innocent, could reflect the experience of many people. Job was not wrong to question God about his suffering. It seems the author chose not to give a clear reason for Job's pain. This might be because suffering is mysterious and unavoidable. Also, knowing the exact reason might not help, as it could be more personal opinion than a clear truth. Therefore, the writer leaves the mystery of suffering open for the reader to explore. The key message is that God remains in control, not as the one who causes evil, but as the one who is present and faithful during times of suffering.

Responding to suffering is not about escaping reality or blindly blaming God, as is often assumed. Instead, it reflects a mature and thoughtful approach to pain. Still, many people continue to hold the belief that both good and evil come from God. Within this view, suffering becomes a way to deepen one's faith and is often interpreted as a hidden blessing. This idea is partly based on 1 Peter 3:14, which says, "But even if you should suffer for righteousness' sake, you are blessed. And do not be afraid of their threats, nor be troubled." Choosing not to react without much thought or with anger in the face of suffering is often seen as submitting to God's will, a quiet trust in His purpose, even when it remains unclear.

Job's experience shows that innocent suffering is complex and often beyond human understanding. The themes of endurance, hope, and trust in God that emerge in Job find a clear continuity in the New Testament. Figures like Paul encounter unexplained trials yet rely on God's grace, demonstrating that suffering remains a space where faith is tested, refined, and strengthened. In both contexts, suffering is not simply a punishment or a problem to solve; it becomes an arena in which God's presence, faithfulness, and sustaining power are experienced, pointing forward to the profound reassurance found in passages such as 2 Corinthians 12:9.

3.4 Job's Response to Suffering in the Light of 2 Cor 12:9

The depth of pain and suffering that Job endured was so severe[48] that it could easily drive a person to suicidal thoughts or even lead to a severe mental and emotional collapse. Such suffering is not only physical but deeply spiritual and existential. However, the author of the book of Job chooses to focus not on the overwhelming weight of Job's agony, but on a significant and powerful dimension of his response: hope. In the midst of unimaginable loss and affliction, Job clings to God in hope.

The writer of the book of Job presents a unique aspect of Job's character in chapter 19, highlighting an eschatological dimension of the Christian faith: hope and integrity. As a human being, Job expresses a strong sense of hopelessness (19:1–12), revealing his emotional and mental pain. At the same time, from a faith perspective, Job puts his hope in

---

[48] Job's suffering was immense. He lost his children, was struck with a painful skin disease, and lived with a wife who was also grieving. His brothers did not support him. His acquaintances, relatives, and close friends turned against him and abandoned him. His servants treated him like a stranger and showed him no respect. He became repulsive to his own family, and even young children despised him (cf. Job 19:3, 13–20).

God. The author carefully portrays these two sides of a believer: first, Job's honest reaction from human weakness in a hopeless situation (19:1–12), and second, Job's response through faith in the same situation. This is clearly seen when Job declares, "For I know that my Redeemer lives" (19:25), which reflects a strong hope in God despite everything he has lost.

Job's hope in his Redeemer (גֹּאֵל, *ga'al*) stands in sharp contrast to his current condition of suffering and despair. The word ga'al, used by the writer, does not refer to a redeemer from sin, but rather to one who restores honour and defends the rights of someone wronged unjustly. The writer intentionally presents God as the Redeemer who will bring justice for Job, not necessarily in this life alone, but even beyond death. This is made clear in Job's bold confession: "And He shall stand at last on the earth" (19:25b), and "after my skin is destroyed, this I know, that in my flesh I shall see God" (19:26). These verses show that Job's faith reaches forward into a future hope; a hope that even if he dies, his Redeemer will stand and defend his cause. The goal of Job's faith, therefore, is not merely relief from suffering, but full justification. The writer's message is that God, as (גֹּאֵל,

ga'al), is the One in whom an innocent sufferer can trust for justice and restoration even beyond the grave.[49]

The narrative of Job presents hope as the foundation of the entire narrative, placing it above the search for immediate justice, explanation, or answers. While questions of fairness, truth, and understanding are present throughout the book, they are not the central focus. Instead, the author emphasises that genuine hope in God precedes and sustains the pursuit of all other resolutions. It is this hope that gives meaning to Job's endurance.[50] Thus, Job dealt with suffering with hope, which led him to see justification and restoration.

The Apostle Paul's experience closely mirrors that of Job, particularly in how both men wrestled with deep, unresolved suffering. Paul describes his pain as "a thorn in the flesh" for which he pleaded with the Lord three times to take away (2 Corinthians 12:7-8). Unlike Job, Paul does not specify the nature of his suffering, yet his response reveals a profound theological truth. Instead of removing the suffering, Jesus responds to Paul with the assurance, "My grace is sufficient

---

[49] Cf. James Strahan, *The Book of Job Interpreted*, 176-177.
[50] Cf. Richard Rohr, *Job and the Mystery of Suffering: Spiritual Reflection*, 110.

for you, for My strength is made perfect in weakness" (2 Corinthians 12:9). This is not to say that Paul's concept of grace supersedes the hope of Job. Instead, it complements it.

Paul's concept of grace is not a novelty of the New Testament. As someone deeply grounded in Jewish Scriptures, Paul would have been familiar with the Hebrew word חֵן (chen), often translated as grace, favour, or acceptance.[51] However, what appears in the New Testament as χάρις (charis), meaning "grace," carries a deeper meaning. The word χάρις (charis) deepens our understanding of God's mercy and kindness, who keeps us, strengthens us, moreover nurtures Christians in faith, knowledge, and affection, and inspires Christians to exercise the Christian virtues.[52]

Paul recognises that suffering is an inevitable part of the Christian life. Suffering is not something Christians can escape, nor seen as a hindrance to our faith. Unlike some who respond to suffering with bitterness or by turning away

---

[51] Cf. Warren Baker, "חֵן," in *The Complete Word Study Dictionary: Old Testament* (Chattanooga: AMG Publishers, 2003), 354.

[52] Cf. James Strong, *The Exhaustive Concordance of the Bible: Showing Every Word of the Text of the Common English Version of the Canonical Books, and Every Occurrence of Each Word in Regular Order*, electronic ed. (Ontario: Woodside Bible Fellowship., 1996), G5485.

from God, Paul accepts it as a part of the journey of faith. He does not view suffering as a contradiction to God's presence but as a context in which God's grace and strength are made manifest. In 2 Corinthians 12:9, Paul recounts the words of Christ: "My grace is sufficient for you, for My strength is made perfect in weakness." This verse not only emphasises grace but also introduces power, and significantly, it places power in weakness. The use of the preposition "in" before "weakness" is critical. It does not suggest that weakness causes power, or that it is a tool God uses to activate power. Instead, it points to a temporal relationship; power is present in the moment of weakness. Weakness, then, is not instrumental but coincidental; it is the setting in which divine strength is revealed.[53]

---

[53] Cf. Paul Raj, "My Grace is Sufficient for You (2 Cor 12:9): Grace vs Boasting in St Paul," in *My Way or God's Way?* eds. Francis Gonsalves, Arjen Tete, Dinesh Braganza (Noida: JDV, 2018), 155.

Conclusion

The story of Job shows that innocent suffering is a real part of life. Even those who have done nothing wrong can face deep pain and loss, as Job did. His suffering was not a punishment from God, nor the result of evil plans. It was part of the human experience. However, in all this, Job held on to hope. He trusted in his Redeemer, confident that God would ultimately save him, defend him, and bring justice, even if that restoration came after his death. His story reminds us that suffering does not always have an explanation, but faith can provide strength and perspective in the midst of it.

This theme continues in the New Testament with Paul, who endured his own mysterious struggles, his "thorn in the flesh," yet found God's grace and strength sufficient for him. Job's story, alongside Pauline insight, portrays a mature Christian approach to suffering: one that neither denies pain nor reduces it to a mere test of faith. Suffering is acknowledged in its full human depth, yet it becomes a context in which believers encounter God's presence, trust in His justice, and cultivate hope that extends beyond immediate circumstances.

In this light, the message is clear: faith does not eliminate suffering, but it places suffering within the hands of a faithful God who is present with us, even when we cannot understand why we suffer.

General Conclusion

This book has focused on the reality of innocent suffering, a question that has troubled believers across every era and culture. The Book of Job, though written long ago, still speaks powerfully into our modern world. It offers a lens through which we can reflect on suffering that is undeserved, confusing, and painful.

The classic question remains: if God is all-powerful and all-knowing, why do the innocent suffer? Why do hardship and loss strike those who have done nothing wrong? Why do children bear burdens they did not choose? These are not merely philosophical questions. They are the cries of real people in moments of despair. Often, we are more concerned with the why than the how. Yet, the more important question may be how we should respond to suffering.

Suffering appears in many forms. It can be physical, emotional, or both. For the purpose of this study, it is helpful to distinguish three kinds of suffering. First, there is suffering that results from our own choices, whether intentional or accidental. Second, there is innocent suffering, which is neither earned nor provoked but is imposed by forces beyond our control. Third, there is sacrificial suffering, where a person willingly suffers for the sake of others. It is the second category, innocent suffering, that most challenges our theology and unsettles our faith.

In exploring Job, this work has not attempted to provide a complete explanation for suffering. Instead, it has sought to offer insights from Job's story that can guide us in times when suffering is unwarranted and unexplained. Job is a dramatic and poetic work, deeply rooted in the worldview of the ancient world. It presents several common explanations for suffering, such as retribution, divine testing, and correction. Yet the story itself challenges these assumptions. If we read it literally, we are faced with troubling implications: God appears to cause suffering or to allow it for a divine debate. Job's friends insist that he must have sinned, but their conclusions are ultimately rejected by God. This exposes the limitations of simplistic theological explanations.

The writer of Job confronts the dominant beliefs of his time, particularly the idea that suffering always comes as a consequence of sin. Job refuses to accept that his suffering is deserved. He does not pretend to understand why he suffers, but he refuses to blame God or deny God's goodness. Instead, he laments honestly, wrestles with divine silence, and holds on to hope in a living Redeemer who will vindicate him.

This vision of a Redeemer becomes the turning point in Job's experience. Job does not claim to have a full understanding. What he does claim is faith in a just God who will restore his honour. His hope is not simply for relief, but for justice and restoration. In this, the New Testament's message of grace and endurance finds a meaningful echo. Paul, too, knows suffering. Yet he anchors his endurance in the sufficiency of God's grace and the sustaining power of Christ. For Paul, this power is revealed through the cross and resurrection, where death itself is defeated, and God's saving purpose is made known. As he declares in 1 Corinthians 15, it is Christ's victory over death that gives meaning, hope, and perseverance to present suffering.

Thus, the Book of Job does not provide a systematic theology of suffering. It offers a journey through suffering. It invites us to live with the mystery, to trust without full answers, and to hold on to hope even in darkness. Job's story teaches that faith does not require full explanation, but it does require trust.

Innocent suffering cannot be explained or justified through retribution, correction, or divine glory. In our modern context, especially for victims of violence or injustice, such explanations are not only insufficient but can be deeply harmful. To suggest that suffering is always a punishment or a necessary tool for God's glory is to misrepresent the God revealed in Scripture.

The Book of Job affirms that suffering is sometimes unexplainable. It also reveals that faith does not demand full understanding. What it calls for is courageous trust in the Redeemer, a hope that does not give up, and a recognition that God's grace is sufficient even in the darkest valleys. Therefore, while suffering remains inevitable, our task is not simply to explain it. Our task is to walk alongside those who suffer, to echo their pain, and to show the compassion of Christ.

Bibliography

Books:

Ash, C. *Job: The Wisdom of the Cross.* Edited by R. Kent Hughes. Illinois: Crossway, 2014.

Best, E. *Second Corinthians. Interpretation: A Bible Commentary for Teaching and Preaching.* Atlanta: John Knox Press, 1987.

Black, A. B., and Mark C. 1 & 2 Peter: The College Press NIV Commentary. Joplin: College Press Publishing, 1998.

Elliott, J. H. 1 Peter: A New Translation with Introduction and Commentary. London: Yale University Press, 2008.

Geisler, N. L. A *Popular Survey of the Old Testament.* Grand Rapids: Baker, 2007.

Grant, O., and Philip W. Comfort. *Cornerstone Biblical Commentary.* Vol. 13. Illinois: Tyndale House Publishers, 2007.

Hartley, J. E. *The Book of Job.* Grand Rapids: Wm. B. Eerdmans Publishing Co., 1988.

Hooks, S. M. *Job*. Joplin: College Press Pub., 2006.

Janzen, J. G. Job. *Interpretation: A Bible Commentary for Teaching and Preaching*. Atlanta: John Knox Press, 1985.

Lewis, C. S. *The Problem of Pain*. New York: Macmillan Publishing Co., 1978.

Perkins, P. *First and Second Peter, James, and Jude. Interpretation: A Bible Commentary for Teaching and Preaching*. Louisville: John Knox Press, 1995.

Reyburn, W. D. *A Handbook on the Book of Job*. New York: United Bible Societies, 1992.

Robinson, H. W. *Suffering Human and Divine*. New York: The Macmillan Company, 1939.

Rohr, R. *Job and the Mystery of Suffering: Spiritual Reflection*. New York: The Crossroad Publishing Co., 2013.

Sper, D. *Why Would a Good God Allow Suffering?* Grand Rapids: RBC Ministries, 2001.

Strahan, J. *The Book of Job Interpreted*. Edinburgh: T. & T. Clark, 1913.

Strong, J. *The Exhaustive Concordance of the Bible: Showing Every Word of the Text of the Common English Version of the Canonical Books, and Every Occurrence of Each Word in Regular Order*. Ontario: Woodside Bible Fellowship, 1996.

The Ante-Nicene Fathers: Fathers of the Third and Fourth Century. Edited by Alexander Roberts, James Donaldson, and Arthur Cleveland Coxe. Vol. 7. New York: Cosimo, Inc., 2007.

The Essence of the Old Testament. Edited by Gary Yates and Edward Hindson. Nashville: B&H Academic, 2012.

Why Does God Allow Suffering? Ohio: United Church of God, 2008.

Yardan, J. L. *God and the Challenge of Evil*. USA: LCCiP, 2001.

Articles, Dictionaries, and Journals

Alden, R. L. "Job." In *The New American Commentary*, vol. 11. Nashville: Broadman & Holman Publishers, 2001.

Baker, W., "ברא." In *The Complete Word Study Dictionary: Old Testament*. Chattanooga: AMG Publishers, 2003.

________. "חֵן." In *The Complete Word Study Dictionary: Old Testament*. Chattanooga: AMG Publishers, 2003.

________. "עָנָה." In *The Complete Word Study Dictionary: Old Testament*. Chattanooga: AMG Publishers, 2003.

Diehl, U. "Human Suffering as a Challenge for the Meaning of Life." *An International Journal in Philosophy, Religion, Politics, and the Arts* 4, no. 2 (2009).

Guzik, D. *The Enduring Word Commentary Series (Isa-Mal)*. Electronic edition. Is 45:4–7.

MacNicoll, P. A. "Elihu." In *Eerdmans Dictionary of the Bible*, edited by Allen C. Myers, Astrid B. Beck, and David Noel Freedman. Grand Rapids: W.B. Eerdmans, 2000.

Oreopoulos, D. G. "Is There Meaning in Suffering?" In *Humane Medicine* 5, no. 2. (2005).

Parsons, G. W. "Guidelines for Understanding and Proclaiming the Book of Job." *Bibliotheca Sacra* 151 (October–December 1994).

Pope, Marvin H. "Job." In *The Anchor Yale Bible Commentary*, vol. 15. London: Yale University Press, 2008.

Raj, P. "My Grace Is Sufficient for You (2 Cor 12:9): Grace vs Boasting in St Paul." *In My Way or God's Way?*, edited by Francis Gonsalves, Arjen Tete, and Dinesh Braganza. Noida: JDV, 2018.

Simundson, D. J. "Suffering." In *The Anchor Yale Bible Dictionary*, edited by David Noel Freedman, vol. 6. New York: Doubleday, 1996.

Smith, B. D. "Suffering." In *Evangelical Dictionary of Biblical Theology*, edited by Walter A. Elwell and Walter A. Elwell. Grand Rapids: Baker Book House, 1997.

Wallace, R. S. "Suffering." In *New Bible Dictionary*, edited by I. Howard Marshall and D. R. W. Wood. Leicester, England: InterVarsity Press, 1996.

Waters, L. J. "Reflections on Suffering from the Book of Job." *Bibliotheca Sacra* 154 (October–December 1997).

Zodhiates, S. "Παιδεία." In *The Complete Word Study Dictionary: New Testament*. Chattanooga, TN: AMG Publishers, 2000.

Internet Resources

Leikind, Bernard. "The Mystery of Evil and Suffering." *TheHumanist.com.* Accessed May 29, 2018. http://thehumanist.com/magazine/may-june-2010/commentary/the-mystery-of-evil-and-suffering.

Silverstein, H. Robert. "How Virtually All Diseases Occur." *The Preventive Medicine Center.* Accessed May 22, 2018. http://www.thepmc.org/2010/04/how-virtually-all-diseases-occur/.

"Evil and Suffering." *Humanism for Schools.* Accessed May 22, 2018. http://www.humanismforschools.org.uk/pdfs/evil%20and%20suffering.pdf.